Splash

I LOVE BEING a Raindrop!

Rebecca Kidd and JulieBelle Ash

Artwork by Irina Bulgaru

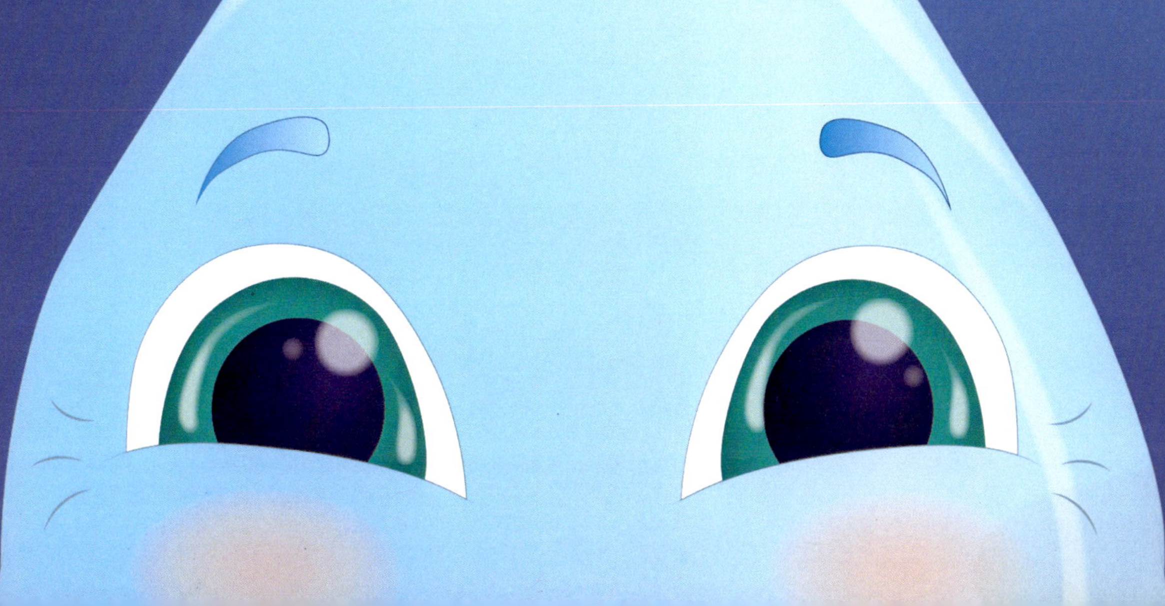

SPLASH, I LOVE BEING A RAINDROP!

www.splashtheraindrop.com

Artwork by Irina Bulgaru
Photography by JulieBelle Ash and Rebecca Kidd,
except Water Wheel photo taken by PapaKaster / Nathan
Art Direction by Jean Bell
Layout & Design by Ty Andrews
Published by Conscious Kids Network, Stone Mountain, GA
www.consciouskidsnetwork.com

Available on Amazon.com
For bulk orders contact BookLogix at:
customerservice@apexbm.com
(470) 239-8552

ISBN: 978-0-9862799-6-6
ISBN: 978-1-5043-7186-5 (e)
Library of Congress Control Number: 2017907233
2nd Edition December 2017

"The waters literally 'sang' and added to the music of Earth's beautiful atmosphere."
~The Gnosis and the Law

Dedication

To the children and grandchildren of our families and the world, to the child within us all, and to every precious drop of water everywhere!

Acknowledgements

Love and Gratitude... To Jean Bell and Ty Andrews of Conscious Kids Network for their joyful & loving guidance, support, insights and creative gifts to bring this book into BEing; and to Irina Bulgaru for bringing Splash to life in her delightful artwork.

Special Appreciation

To PapaKaster / Nathan for his water wheel photo; to Peggy Tibbetts, Padgett McFeely and Haven Stillwater for their creative suggestions; to Dr. Masaru Emoto for his inspiring work with water; and to Mo Willems who inspired us to combine photos with artwork through his example in *Knuffle Bunny*.

far, far away in a part of the universe where the sun shines and the stars sparkle, lives a raindrop named Splash. He is practicing every day to prepare for his great Earth adventure.

While he waits to visit Earth, Splash plays raindrop games with his friends. Playing hide and seek in a rainstorm is one of his favorite games. He also loves bursting out of a blustery thundercloud or falling softly as a gentle spring rain.

The games are fun, but he wonders, *When will my Earth adventures begin*?

Then one day, his teacher calls him away from the games to ask, "Are you ready to be a part of something great on Earth?"

Splash shivers excitedly and shouts, "YES!" He feels a flutter. This is the real thing, no longer make-believe. He asks his teacher, "Will I be able to make a difference, even though I am so small?"

The teacher explains, "Even though you may feel small, it is your important mission to carry water to Earth. Always remember who you are and how special you are."

All the selected raindrops gather together to form a cloud that floats toward Earth. Splash giggles as a wind spirit tickles him and guides the raindrops closer to a beautiful mountain peak.

"Oooooo!" Splash exclaims. He wonders how close they will get before they each drop to the ground. As Splash gently falls he whispers, "This is so much more fun than the games."

Splash feels warm rays of the sun shining through him. Suddenly, he sees a dazzling array of colors shimmering through all the raindrops. A child shouts, "Look at the beautiful rainbow, Daddy!"

Smiling, Splash cries, **"I love being a raindrop bringing beauty to the Earth!"**

Splash heads for a lush, green meadow. He gleefully lands on the soft, pink petal of a flower. He feels it straighten and open a little wider as it blossoms. The flower says, “Thank you for falling on me. I felt dry and needed a drink.”

Splash rolls down the petal to its edge. **“I love being a raindrop helping flowers to grow and blossom!”**

Letting go, Splash drops to the grass. "Wheeee!" he squeals joyfully as he slides down the slope to the creek. Happily he joins the other raindrops in a fast-flowing stream. He wonders where they are going so fast.

Splash dashes around rocks, logs, and trees in the water. Then he feels a great WOOOSH and tumbles over a waterfall into a lake.

Splash sees and hears children laugh as they play in the water. He dances in and around their legs. Shrieking with delight, he flies through the air! A child shouts, "It is so *fun* splashing and playing in the water!"

Splash giggles, **"I love being a raindrop playing with children!"**

“Come on. We’re going to the far side of the lake,” his droplet friends yell. Splash joins them as they ride high on the waves.

As the current pulls them, Splash feels a shiver of anticipation. He knows something big is about to happen.

DANGER!
RAINDROPS ONLY!

A gigantic water wheel whirls. Rolling and spinning through the wheel, Splash feels a sudden jolt of electricity. "Hey, what are you doing to me?" he asks the big wheel.

The wheel replies, "I spin around and generate electric power to light people's homes and keep them warm. I couldn't do it without you. Thank you!"

"Wow!" says Splash. **"I love being a raindrop, helping to give people light and warmth!"**

He sprays off the wheel and spills into a dark, round pipe. Splash wonders where it will take him. He relaxes and allows himself to be carried along.

Splash sees a light ahead. Gushing out into big bubbles of soap, he floats around a rubber ducky. A child giggles with delight.

Splash is picked up on a soapy washcloth and rubbed all over the child's dirty face. *This feels a little rough and squishy at the same time,* Splash marvels as he slides back into the tub.

The mother lifts her child out of the bathtub and exclaims, "Look how clean you've gotten with the soap and water, and how wonderful you smell!"

"I love being a raindrop helping people feel clean and fresh!" Splash sings.

After gurgling round and round through more pipes and exploring some curious places...

Splash feels a bump.

Whirling and twirling into backflips, and twisting high into the air, he shoots out of a garden hose and lands on a big green leaf.

A grandmother bends down and picks a sugar snap pea from its vine. She explains to her grandchild, “Look how the water helps our garden vegetables to grow.”

The grandchild bites into the fresh pea and announces, “This tastes so juicy and sweet! Grandma, let’s thank all water everywhere!”

Hearing the grandchild’s words, Splash feels transformed and softly whispers, **“I love being a raindrop helping food to grow!”**

Splash sighs happily as he reviews all of his adventures. He remembers the beautiful rainbow, the thirsty flower, the splashing children, the gigantic wheel, the soapy bathtub, and the vegetable garden. "Wow!" Splash exclaims, "I *have* made a difference here on Earth."

Suddenly, his teacher's words echo in his mind. Splash realizes that even though he is only one small raindrop, he is a very special part of something a lot bigger.

"I really love BEING a Raindrop!"

Welcome Home!

At that moment the sun illumines him once again with rainbow colors. Splash feels a delightful change within. He glistens and becomes lighter, almost invisible. He floats higher and higher into the sky.

As he evaporates, Splash knows that he is going home where the sun shines and the stars sparkle. With his mission complete, his heart fills with gratitude. Splash is eager to see his teacher and friends again. He is excited to share stories of his adventures.

Feeling happy and content, Splash the Raindrop knows that someday he will visit Earth again.

Explore the Magic and Wonder of

SPLASH AND WATER

WHAT DO YOU KNOW ABOUT WATER AND...

- rainbows
- flowers
- splashing
- baths
- waterwheels
- gardens
- evaporation

What else do you know about water?

WONDERING ABOUT SPLASH AND YOU

Why does Splash love being a raindrop?
What do you love about being you?

How does water help us?
How can we help water?

How can one drop of water make a difference?
How can you make a difference?

Enjoying the Fun and Magic of WATER

- Draw or Paint a Picture of...
  ~ your favorite adventure that Splash has on Earth.
  ~ how water is used and enjoyed on Earth.
  ~ your favorite adventure with water.
  ~ a rainbow with the colors in the order that they appear in real life. Why do they appear this way?

- Experiment with water. How are waves made? Why do some things float and other things sink? How does water seem magical?

- Move like you are water in a stream, on a wave, in the ocean, in the air, in a cloud, falling to Earth, in a rainbow, in a bubble bath.

- Investigate more fun facts about water online with your favorite adult.

Fun Facts About WATER

- The scientific symbol for water is H_2O, meaning water contains 2 atoms of hydrogen and 1 atom of oxygen.
- Water can be a solid, liquid, or gas.
- In the water cycle, Earth's water evaporates and condenses into clouds, then precipitates back to Earth. This repeats over again and again.
- Water covers about 70% of the Earth's surface.

- Less than 3% of all water on Earth is fresh water.
- Your body is made up of about two-thirds water.
- Pure water has no smell and no taste.
- Drinking clean water is essential to human life. It helps you stay hydrated, flush out toxins in the body, and keep your mouth and teeth clean.

About the Authors

"We illumine the heart and mind
with the magic and wonder of the Universe
through joyful, uplifting stories that honor All."

Rebecca is a Healing Touch Practitioner and an ordained minister. She's a mother and grandmother who loves to laugh and play. She has participated in and facilitated many Team Building and Communication trainings. She delights in others discovering their greatness. She wrote and published *Dear Womenfriends*, a powerful pocket book of wisdom. She believes in honor and respect for our earth and all of nature, which led to the inspiration for this story.

JulieBelle has a Master's Degree in Education, and from many years of teaching and parenting she knows that every child brings a special gift to the world. Through inspiring literature, it is her joy and honor to help children enliven these gifts! Her published articles, workshops, camps, classes and sessions all focus upon empowering and uplifting the Spirit. She loves capturing nature's magic through the lens of her Salida, Colorado home.

Conscious Kids Network (CKN) is a children/youth publishing service that provides life-enhancing tools through books, music and entertainment. CKN's mission is to inspire youth to live an empowered, happy life. We value providing a multi-media platform that champions young people to express their creativity, embrace their abilities and learn how to deal with life situations effectively.

For more book publications and information, visit
www.consciouskidsnetwork.com